THE BLACK CROOK

The Black Crook

THE BLACK CROOK

The 1866 Musical Extravaganza

Complete Libretto

By Charles M. Barras

Theatre Arts Press
Historical Libretto Series

The Black Crook

This libretto published from primary sources and other historical records.

For a complete list of titles from the Historical Libretto Series, visit Musical--Librettos.com

Copyright © 2015 Theatre Arts Press

All rights reserved. No part of this publication may be reproduced or transmitted in any form or by any means, now known or yet be to invented, electronic or mechanical, including photocopy, recording, or any information storage and retrieval system.

Printed in the United States of America
9 8 7 6 5 4 3 2 1

The Black Crook opened at Niblo's Garden, New York on September 12, 1866 with the following cast:

Rodolphe......................... George Boniface
Amina.............................. Rose Morton
Dame Barbara................ Mary Wells
Count Wolfenstein......... J. W. Blaisdell
Von Puffengruntz.......... J.G. Burnett
Hertzog........................... C. H. Morton
Stalacta........................... Annie Kemp Bowler
Greppo............................ George Atkins
Wolfgar........................... E. Barry
Zamiel............................. E. B. Holmes
Skuldawelp..................... Mr. Rendle
Bruno.............................. F. Ellis
Casper............................. H. Weaver
Carline............................ Milly Cavendish
Rosetta............................ Miss C. Whitlock

The Black Crook

Cast of Characters

Rodolphe
Amina
Dame Barbara
Count Wolfenstein
Von Puffengruntz
Hertzog, the Black Crook
Stalacta
Greppo
Wulfgar
Zamiel
Skuldawelp
Redglare
Bruno
Casper
Jan
Carline
Rosetta

Villagers, Peasants, Choresters, Guards, Attendants, Fairies, Amphibeas, Gnomes, Infernals, Sprites, Naiads, Submarine Monsters

The Black Crook

Act One

Scene 1

A quiet valley at the foot of the Hartz Mountains, 1600.

Cottage of Dame Barbara with practicable upper window and balcony. Broken water and rustic stone bridge or long rocky trail piece with platform backed by an extended range of hills or mountain spurs above which light clouds appear, illuminated by the reflected light of the moon.

Shortly after rise of curtain the moonbeams grow faint and the ruddy glow of the rising sun diffuses itself over the clouds and horizon.

Music at rise of curtain. Enter RODOLPHE, a poor artist. He descends, comes forward and after looking cautiously around claps his hands three times beneath the window. The upper window opens and AMINA, his betrothal, appears on balcony.

AMINA. Surely I heard his well-known signal. Hist, who's there?

RODOLPHE. Tis I, Rodolphe!

AMINA. Rodolphe! Hush speak low, if my foster mother still sleeps, I will join you.

> *(She retires. Music. RODOLPHE goes upstage and looks cautiously off, then comes down. AMINA enters from cottage.)*

AMINA. *(Throwing herself into his arms.)* Rodolphe!

RODOLPHE. My own!

AMINA. When did you return?

RODOLPHE. 'Twas past midnight: although wearied and footsore I could not sleep until I had seen you.

AMINA. Oh, how wearily the days and nights have passed since you left me! What kept you so long?

RODOLPHE. Ill fortune, Amina. After reaching Gottingen and finding no purchaser for my picture I heard that there was a wealthy traveler at Cassel, collecting works of art. I had but four silver florins in my pocket yet I hopefully set out to meet him. After journeying five whole days I arrived at Cassel only to find that the traveler had departed two days before.

AMINA. And your beautiful picture—upon which so much of our future was built—you have brought it back?

RODOLPHE. No. Crushed in my last hope to obtain the means necessary to our union I left it with a remorseless agent for a pittance barely sufficient for subsistence during my journey homeward, and here I am without a single guilder in my pocket! And what is worse if I fail to redeem my pledge at the end of two months it is lost to me forever.

AMINA. *(Aside.)* Poor, dear Rodolphe, he knows not the worst— the heaviest blow is yet to come. How shall I break it to him? *(Aloud.)* Dear Rodolphe, my great joy at seeing you made me forget for a moment that which I fear to tell you.

(The moonlight begins to fade and the horizon grow ruddy with the rising sun.)

RODOLPHE. Fear to tell me! Speak, what has happened?

AMINA. Be calm and listen. Last week I attended the festival of St. John, in company with the other members of the village choir. Upon raising my eyes after we had finished the anthem I found a dark, strange man gazing upon me. A moment after he quitted the spot I enquired who he was and learned that it was the Count Wolfenstein, the all powerful lord of this wide domain.

RODOLPHE. Well.

AMINA. Although I met his gaze but for a moment, I felt that it boded evil to me—to us.

RODOLPHE. Evil! Evil to us?

AMINA. Yes, evil, Rodolphe, nor were my fears idle, the next day brought him here to our humble abode—he told my foster- mother that he loved me.

RODOLPHE. *(Starting.)* Loved!—You?

AMINA. Yes, and that we should no longer dwell in obscurity— that we should be removed to the castle—that masters should be provided for my suitable education, and in a year I should take the place of the late Countess of Wolfenstein.

RODOLPHE. And Dame Barbara?

AMINA. Joyfully consented. This very day is set apart for our removal. The escort will be here at sunrise.

RODOLPHE. And you, Amina, You—?

AMINA. I supplicated, wept, remonstrated, but you know, dear Rodolphe, I am powerless.

RODOLPHE. *(Vehemently.)* By Heaven, you shall not go.

AMINA. Hush, be calm, dear Rodolphe.

> *(DAME BARBARA, Amina's foster mother, appears on the balcony.)*

RODOLPHE. I say you shall not! Were he twenty times more potent I would oppose his power to the last.

BARBARA. Eh, what, varlet, hussy, only wait till I get down! *(Music. She disappears from balcony and enters from door.)* What, jade, ingrate! How dare you? Is this your gratitude? Where is your pride? Now, the most noble Countess of Wolfenstein that is to be meeting young men in secret and on the very day of your betrothal. Oh, if his high mightiness the Count should find it out!

AMINA. But mother—

BARBARA. Not a word—how dare you? In with you, into the house, I say! *(Forces her into the cottage, closes the door, then turns to RODOLPHE.)* So, beggar, you've come back have you? How dare you show your unlucky face here at such a time as this! I had hoped you had fallen into the hands of the conscript officers and gone for a soldier, or better still, been carried off by the demons of the Brocken.

RODOLPHE. And yet you see I've escaped both. Hark ye, dame. I love Amina, she loves me, you yourself promised that she should be mine as soon as I could command a hundred silver crowns.

BARBARA. Pah, that was before I knew her value, but now that I do know it and others know it too, I've changed my mind. But where are the hundred crowns? Where's the fortune you were to get for your great painting? I warrant me you haven't got a single groschen of it. Come, let me see the hundred crowns.

RODOLPHE. My picture is not yet sold.

BARBARA. Ha, ha! Didn't I say so, not yet sold eh? Here's a pretty fellow, that would take a young girl from her comfortable home, a good bed, sweet milk and egg-pudding, to lodge her on pea-straw, and feed her at best on black bread and sour cheese. Oh, was there ever such villainy?

RODOLPHE. Nay, but listen to me.

BARBARA. Not a word. Begone! Do you think people of quality have nothing to do but listen to beggars complaints, and above all at such a time as this? Begone, I say, this is to be a festival day, the maidens of the village will be here anon; the grand escort will be here, headed by the Count's chamberlain, Aye, and his Lordship the Count himself will be here, to bear the Countess that is to be and her right honorable foster-mother that is to be to the Castle. *(Music.)* Hark, here come the villagers already: Out of the way I say.

(Pushes him rudely aside, goes up and looks offstage. RODOLPHE retires into the arbor. Enter lively from back, FEMALE VILLAGERS with garlands, followed by MALES, two of whom bear a rustic chair, festooned with flowers. They descend and come forward, greeting DAME BARBARA. The sun appears above one of the spurs of the Mountains.)

BARBARA. Ah, you are early, friends.

CARLINE. Yes, but not earlier than the sun, for see, it is already peeping over the great toe of the Brocken. But where's Amina?

BARBARA. *(Drawing herself up.)* The Countess that is to be is preparing to receive his lordship the Count. But never mind her ladyship, enjoy yourselves until she is ready. Here, Casper, here I am, come with me and bring some refreshments while I help to prepare her ladyship

(Goes into the cottage followed by CASPER and JAN. The two latter re-enter with white cloth, wine, fruits, etc. which they arrange on the table beneath the tree.)

CARLINE. Bless me, how grand Dame Barbara has grown, to be sure. If she goes on at this rate the wide halls of the grand old Castle of Wolfenstein will be a world too small to hold her. I hope this piece of good fortune will not make such a fool of dear 'Mina

ROSETTA. I don't understand this, I thought 'Mina was betrothed to the handsome young painter Rodolphe, what ever could have become of him?

CARLINE. Oh, 'tis said he has gone for a soldier. But come, while 'Mina is making ready let us rehearse our Festival Dance.

(Music: Grand Garland Dance by principals and full Ballet, during which the Males gather around the table and eat and drink. After dance, BARBARA re-enters extravagantly dressed, wearing a monstrous cap ridiculously trimmed.)

BARBARA. There! Having completed her ladyships toilet I have attended to my own, and, if I know anything about dress, I flatter myself that my appearance would do honor to any occasion.

(Displays herself.)

CARLINE. *(Aside to ROSETTA.)* Mercy on us, was there ever such a fright! Why she looks for all the world like a great horned owl dressed up in the cast-off finery of a peacock. Ha, ha, ha, Did you ever? Observe me tickle the old buzzard. *(Aloud and with affected admiration.)* Why! Dame Barbara, is that you?

BARBARA. *(Drawing herself up.)* Of course it is, child. Who else should it be? *(Aside.)* I knew I should make them open their eyes.

CARLINE. Why you've almost taken away my breath. I declare, Dame, you're looking gorgeous—so young and girlish too. Indeed, if I were 'Mina—I beg pardon I mean her ladyship, I wouldn't care to have you in the way when his lordship, the Count, arrives.

BARBARA. And why not, pray?

CARLINE. Because I should consider you a dangerous rival.

BARBARA. Nonsense, girl, you don't think so?

CARLINE. Indeed, Dame Barbara, I was never more serious in my life.

(Laughingly confers with ROSETTA and VILLAGERS.)

BARBARA. It's strange I never noticed it before, but that girl Carline's a very sensible person. *(Music.)* Ah, here comes the escort!

(All go up and look off right. RODOLPHE glides from the arbor into the cottage unobserved. Enter from back, and descending VON PUFFENGRUNTZ, bearing the wand of office, He is preceded by two servants of the Count's household, as he comes down the Male VILLAGERS take off their caps and the females curtsey.)

VON PUFF. *(With pompous condescension.)* Be covered, good people, be covered; the air of the valley is yet damp. We never insist upon ceremony at the expense of health. *(Aside.)* Ahem. It is the true policy of greatness to occasionally waive a point of etiquette in dealing with inferiors.

BARBARA. What a courtly gentleman!

VON PUFF. What an imposing female!

BARBARA. *(Curtseying.)* Your Excellency is welcome.

VON PUFF. *(Bowing.)* I cannot be mistaken. I was just about to inquire, but that stately presence and graceful dignity tell me that I am addressing Madam Barbara.

BARBARA. *(Curtseying.)* Oh, sir. *(Aside.)* How one's manner will betray one, I always said I belonged to a higher sphere.

VON PUFF. I come, Madam, by the Count's order to announce that the cavalcade has arrived and is now resting on the plateau, beyond the ravine. His lordship will be here presently and in person conduct your fair foster daughter to her palfrey, that waits without, impatient for the honor to be mounted by her.

BARBARA. *(Curtseying.)* Oh, sir, his lordship is so considerate. But may I inquire if I have been thought of? And I also to be provided with a becoming escort? Is there any palfrey without impatient for the honor to be ridden by me?

VON PUFF. That shall be my privilege

BARBARA. *(Astonished.)* Eh!

VON PUFF. That is I have charged myself with the especial honor of being your escort.

BARBARA. *(Curtseying very low.)* Oh!

(Music.)

VON PUFF. He comes! Room there for his lordship.

> *(VILLAGERS range themselves to receive the COUNT who enters at back, crosses and comes down left preceded by GUARDS and followed by WULFGAR and BRUNO. When down VILLAGERS shout and wave their caps.)*

WOLFENSTEIN. Salutation to the good dame Barbara.

BARBARA. *(Curtseying very low.)* Oh, your lordship!

WOLFENSTEIN. And how fares your lovely charge?

BARBARA. Well, may it please your lordship, quite well, a little nervous from over-anxiety to see your lordship, but that is quite natural with us poor silly things. I suffered dreadfully in that way when my poor dear, dead and gone Christopher courted me. Many and many a time—

WOLFENSTEIN. *(Impatiently interrupting her.)* But the fair Amina.

BARBARA. Is quite ready and dying to see you—I will present her to your lordship at once.

> *(She is going into the cottage when RODOLPHE appears and comes forward, leading AMINA by the hand. CHORD)*

RODOLPHE. Allow me Dame Barbara, to do the honors.

ALL THE VILLAGERS. Rodolphe!

(Picture of astonishment.)

RODOLPHE. My lord Count Wolfenstein, permit me, Rodolphe Werner, a poor artist, to present to you Amina, foster-daughter to Dame Barbara, a free maiden of the valley and my affianced bride.

WOLFENSTEIN. Who is this madman?

BARBARA. N-n-n-n-n-n-nobody, your Lordship, that is a poor, weak simpleton who imagines he is betrothed to every girl in the village. As your lordship truly says, a madman.

The Black Crook

VON PUFF. A madman! Mercy on us, we shall all be murdered. Seize him, secure him, somebody, everybody.

(Music. WULFGAR and BRUNO seize RODOLPHE and after a struggle overpower him. AMINA screams, clings to him for a moment then throws herself at the COUNT'S feet, he raises and passes her to BARBARA, then turns to GUARDS.)

WOLFENSTEIN. Release him. *(They release him.)* His misfortune claims our pity. Let some of his fellows conduct him hence and see that no harm come to him.

RODOLPHE. *(Defiantly.)* My Lord Count—

WOLFENSTEIN. Begone, Sirrah!

CASPER. Come, Rodolphe, come with me. *(Aside.)* Are you indeed mad to brave the tiger in his lair— *(Leads him right.)* Come I say, this is neither time nor place to right your wrong. Be calm, I say, be calm.

RODOLPHE. *(Shaking him by the hand.)* You are right, Casper, you are right. *(Looks scornfully at WOLFENSTEIN.)* Come, my friend, come.

(H exits with CASPER.)

WOLFENSTEIN. *(Aside.)* 'Tis he, the lover. He braves me, too. *(Aloud.)* Wulgar! *(WULFGAR advances. Apart to WULFGAR.)* Track yonder knave, take Bruno with you. Seize him, but let no eye see you, Place him in the secret vault beneath the eastern wing. Once there—you know the rest.

WULFGAR. *(Nods meaningly.)* I understand.

(Gives sign to BRUNO.)

WOLFENSTEIN. Stay not now, it will be noted. When the procession moves then steal away by the upper path.

(WULFGAR nods, turns upstage and confers with BRUNO. WOLFENSTEIN confers with VON PUFFENGRUNTZ at back.)

BARBARA. *(Leading AMINA forward and aside to her)* Silence, on your life, not a word that you have ever seen him before. If the Count were to know—Mercy on me, I tremble to think of it, there wouldn't be a head left on any of our shoulders.

(Birds heard singing till scene closes)

VON PUFF. *(Waving his wand.)* Let the procession move.

(Music. WOLFENSTEIN joins AMINA, Villagers bring forward the festooned chair. WOLFENSTEIN assists AMINA into the seat. The chair is borne by four villagers. The others form in procession. WOLFENSTEIN beside the chair, VON PUFFENGRUNTZ pompously leading BARBARA by the hand. WULFGAR and BRUNO loiter behind and when unobserved steal off right. The procession after making the circuit of the stage ascends the rocks left and crosses right, the VILLAGERS singing the following:)

CHORUS.
Hark, hark, hark!
Hark, the birds with tuneful voices,
Vocal for our lady fair,
And the lips of op'ning flowers
Breathe their incense on the air,
Breathe their incense on the air.
See, see, see,
See the sun in orient splendor
Gilding every glittering spray,
Busy weaving jewelled chaplets
For our lovely Queen of May,
For our lovely Queen of May.
Mark, mark, mark!
Mark the plumes of mighty Brocken
Waving in the fragrant air,
Proudly nodding salutation
To our charming lady fair,
To our charming lady fair.

Curtain

Act One

Scene 2

A dark woody or rocky pass.

Lights half down. Music. Enter WULFGAR and BRUNO.

WULFGAR. So, we've reached the pass a good five minutes before him.

BRUNO. But if he should cross the bridge?

WULFGAR. Aye, if, but he'll not. I watched him from behind "The Devil's Hump" and saw him part company with that lout at the foot of the old cross. I tell you his path lies this way. *(Crosses to left.)* Hark some one comes. *(Looks cautiously off.)* Ha, I was right, 'tis he, quick conceal yourself and when I hood the hawk stand ready to clip his claws.

(Music. WULFGAR conceals himself left, Bruno right. Music. Enter RODOPLHE.)

RODOLPHE. Deeper, let me plunge, deeper still into the heart of the mountains: the light of the sun falls like molten lead on my aching eyeballs. My heart's on fire, my brain is in a whirl, I strive to think, but thought becomes a chaos. Am I awake or is this some horrible dream? Water, water, my throat is flaming. Ha, yonder's a rill trickling from the rock.

(Music. He is going right when WULFGAR who has stolen from his concealment throws a cloak over his head, while BRUNO at the same moment pinions his arms, RODOLPHE struggling violently.)

WULFGAR. Quick, quick, the cord, the cord! He has the strength of a lion. *(BRUNO draws a cord tightly over his arms.)* So, away, away!

(Music. They force RODOLPHE off right.)

Curtain

Act One

Scene 3

Study and laboratory of the Black Crook.

HERTZOG *discovered, seated at table poring over a large cabalistic book.* GREPPO, *pinched and starved asleep on stool before a retort furnace. An* antique lamp illuminates the characters of the book upon the table, upon which is a skull and hour-glass. Music at opening of scene.

HERTZOG. *(Rising in pain and with difficulty, he closes the book and comes forward.)* Vain, vain, some subtitle spell is hovering in the air that mocks my power and makes the charms that once were potent a jabbering idle sound. And shall I yield to this Invisible? I, Hertzog, the Crook, whom men call sorcerer. I, at whose name the strong man trembles and the weak grows faint. I whose life of long, laborious years hath well nigh run its course, gleaning dark knowledge in forbidden paths, shall I now seek the light? My eyes are old and dim and could not brave the glare. No, no, I'll work new mines--new mines, and plumb the depths of darker mysteries still. *(GREPPO snores loudly.)* How now, knave?

GREPPO. *(Starts from his sleep and uses the bellows rapidly at the mouth of the furnace.)*

HERTZOG. Come hither, varlet.

GREPPO. Yes, master.

(He rises from stool, puts down bellows and comes forward, yawning.)

HERTZOG. What, drone, sluggard, snoring again?

GREPPO. N-n-n-no good master, no.

HERTZOG. Out, lying knave. Did I not hear thee snore?

GREPPO. Snore? Aye, granted, but 'twas in thy service, master, much fasting and long watching caused this left rebellious eye to wink, and so I snored to wake it up again.

HERTZOG. Bah! Shuffling loon, thy drowsing comes of overfeeding.

GREPPO. *(Viewing himself.)* Overfeeding? Look I if I were overfed? A scanty chopin of weak sour beer with one poor groschen's worth of musty beans is all the banquet this shrunk belly knows from week to week.

HERTZOG. What, rogue, dost grumble?

GREPPO. No, good master, no.

(Rumbling thunder. Music. Tremolo piano.)

HERTZOG. Ha, the night grows foul. 'Tis all the better, Bring me my cloak and staff

(Thunder.)

GREPPO. *(Bringing forward crutch stick and short, black hooded cloak from nail on flat.)* They are here.

(Places cloak on HERTZOG'S shoulders.)

HERTZOG. *(Drawing the hood over his head.)* So, now thine own.

GREPPO. My cloak: I have none, Master.

HERTZOG. Thy cap.

GREPPO. Mine?

HERZOG. Thine.

(Thunder.)

GREPPO. Oh, Lord, what a night.

(Brings his cap from peg beside the furnace.)

HERTZOG. Bring with thee yonder brazen casket.

GREPPO. Th-the-the brazen casket?

HERTZOG. Aye, echoing fool!

(Thunder.)

GREPPO. *(Tremblingly goes to table and takes casket. Aside.)* The devil's tool-chest. *(Aloud.)* Whither go we, dread master?

HERTZOG. To the Serpents' Glen.

(Loud thunder.)

GREPPO. *(Starting.)* Oh Lord, the Serpents' Glen! Beelzebub's favorite chapel, surely, good master, you would not, and above all on such a night as this? *(Thunder and lightning, the latter showing itself in transparent window.)* Hark how the tempest howls; Strong pines are toppling down the mountain sides. 'Twere certain death to go abroad to night.

HERTZOG. Silence, and follow.

(He goes toward door. Lightning and loud thunder)

GREPPO. *(Has made a movement to follow, starts back trembling violently.)* Master, I cannot!

HERTZOG. *(Turning fiercely.)* What, ingrate, do you rebel?

GREPPO. No, master, no, my spirit's willing, but my legs are weak.

HERTZOG. Wretch, did I not snatch thee drowning from the whirling gulf, bind thy torn limbs with rare medicaments and stanch the current of thy ebbing life that fast was running out?

GREPPO. You did, good master, you did. *(Aside.)* Out of the water into the fire.

HERZOG. Begone! *(Music forte. Throws opon the door. Loud thunder and wind. lightning. GREPPO starts back.)* Fool, begone, I say. *(Seizes and hurls him toward the open door. Heavy thunder and lightning. GREPPO in doorway entreats. HERTZOG raises his staff.)* Away, away!

(Thunder and lightning. HERTZOG and GREPPO exit.)

Curtain

Act One

Scene 4

An apartment in the castle of Wolfenstein.

Low thunder. Lights up.

CARLINE. *(Enters.)* Bless me, what a night to welcome her ladyship that is to be to her new home. I declare the old castele trembles and shakes like a great ship at sea. *(Loud thunder.)* Mercy on us, what a crash! But pshaw, why should I care how the tempest rages without. Am I not safe within, and in rare good luck too? Only to think that I should be chosen from among all the girls in the village to become Amina's companion and own particular waiting maid. Old Hagar, the gypsy fortune teller whose palm I crossed with a new quarter florin last week told me that good fortune awaited me, and sure enough, here it is. Only to think of it, that I, Carline Brenner, who for ten long years have been chained to a stupid spinning wheel day an night should become confidential companion to the future mistress of Wolfenstein. Was there ever such good fortune? I declare, I am so happy I could sing for a month.

(Introduced song and exits.)

Curtain

Act One

Scene 5

A wild glen in the heart of the Brocken.

Perilous rocky pathway leading from above at back. Returning crosses over a rock five feet high right exit, with set blasted tree back of it. Large working raven on limb and vampire doors in trunk. Set rock-piece in center of stage, opposite second grooves, bearing a general resemblance to a rude altar. The whole stage is much broken up with rocky sets, leaving the center back of the altar generally open.

Lights down. Music at opening. HERZOG appears, followed by GREPPO, making several efforts to turn back is checked by HERZOG.

GREPPO. *(Coming forward.)* Oh Lord, what a place. *(Music. The raven croaks, flaps its wings and shows red illuminated eyes. GREPPO starts.)* What's that? *(Turns.)* Twas the croaking of yonder mock-raven, did'st hear, master? 'Tis an evil sign, let's begone.

HERZOG. Silence, fool. Set down the casket.

(He goes up stage.)

GREPPO. I will. *(Sets the casket on ground.)* Thank St. Michael, I'm rid of that pleasant companion. As I have an empty belly and hope some day to have it filled, I could swear before the Burgomaster that when we passed over the bridge of Beelzebub's Nose I heard voices laughing inside that very casket,-saw blue blazes come out of the keyhole and smelt a strong smell of brimstone. *(Music. Raven croaks as before. Looking* *around fearfully.*) Oh Lord, Oh Lord, what a pleasant place for an uninterrupted funeral. Ugh!

HERZOG. Knave.

GREPPO. Master.

HERZOG. Bring hither full.

GREPPO. I obey. *(Aside.)* Here's a chance, if I can only get out of this, may the Fiend singe me if he catches me back. I'd rather be on the raging flood than serve him an hour longer.

(He is about to ascend the rocks.)

HERZOG. Whither go now, varlet?

GREPPO. For fuel, master. This around us is wet with the storm and will not burn. As we came along I noted many dry faggots. I will fetch them. *(Going.)*

HERZOG. Come back. *(GREPPO groans and returns. Pointing right.)* The dead branches of yon blasted larch will serve.

GREPPO. But, master—

HERZOG. Dolt, obey me.

GREPPO. I'm gone.

(He groans and exits. Music. HERZOG goes slowly up to set altar and smites it three times with his stick. Blue flame issues from the top of the altar and continues through the scene. GREPPO re-enters with armload of faggots.)

GREPPO. Here are the faggots, master.

HERZOG. 'Tis well. Feed yonder flame.

GREPPO. A flame! How came we by a flame? I'll swear I brought no tinder-box. More brimstone, I suppose. Oh Lord, oh Lord!

HERZOG. Fool, do as I command.

GREPPO. I fly. *(Music. He goes slowly and timidly up to and behind altar with faggots.)* Now for some devil's cookery.

Herzog. So. Pluck me an inner leaf from yonder adder plant.

(He points to trick plant left.)

GREPPO. I knew it. Vegetable broth.

(Music. He approaches the plant and is about to pluck it when it opens suddenly and discovers a dwarf demon, around whose body in twined a huge green serpent with flaming eyes, distended jaws and forked tongue. As the leaves open the head darts at GREPPO viciously. He starts back, uttering a cry of alarm- the leaves closes.)

HERZOG. Ha! *(Stamps his foot angrily and points to the plant. Same business as above with GREPPO, demon serpent and plant. Chafing.)* So, so. Bring me the green flagon from yonder casket.

(Music. GREPPO goes to casket and raises the lid when fire flashes from the box. He starts back in an agony of fear and crossing site upon the small set rock-pieces, when flames shoot from the stone and springs into the air, uttering a sharp cry of pain.)

HERZOG. *(Enraged.)* Baffled at every turn! Begone, knave, thy presence mars my work.

GREPPO. Most willingly.

(He is about to ascend the rocks.)

HERZOG. Not there. *(GREPPO groans and returns.)* Keep watch without from yonder crag that overhangs the gorge. Should straggling footsteps wend this way, give timely warning.

GREPPO. *(Aside.)* Straggling footsteps! Straggling indeed to be abroad on such a night, and least of all in such a place as this.

HERZOG. Did'st hear me?

GREPPO. I vanish.

(He exits. Music. HERZOG describes a circle and figures on the ground center with his stick, after which the end of the stick ignites and burns with a faint blue flame. He then describes figures in the air, during which latter action he speaks.)

HERZOG. Skuldawelp, familiar, slave of my power, I invoke thee.

(Music. A spectra in filmy draper with death's head, luminous eyes, movable jaw and skeleton hands walks on from right to center. Illuminated by light from calcium.)

SKULDAWELP. Your will.

HERZOG. Break the malignant spells that thwart and mock me. Bind fast my hidden enemies. Restore to me my lost power.

SKULDAWELP. I cannot. An adverse spell has crossed me. My power is spent. All that was mine is thine. Zamiel alone can serve thee.

HERZOG. *(Thinking.)* Zamiel.

SKULDAEWELP. Zamiel!—dismiss me.

HERZOG. *(Waving his staff.)* Begone! *(Music. SKULDAWELP glides off left.)* Zamiel! No, no. I dare not invoke his fearful aid. *(Music tremolo piano.)* I-I. Ha, what tremor's this? My blood grows very cold, my limbs are failing, a film is gathering over my eyes. *(Falls center.)* Can this be death? Death! No, no. I cannot, I will not die. Save me, save, Zamiel, Zamiel! *(Music forte. He drags himself toward the casket, seizes it, rises with difficulty and totters to the altar, at the foot of which he places the casket, opens it and brings forth a packet containing four lesser packets and begins the following incantation:)* By a bloody murder done. Gainst a mother by her son! *(Casts red ingredient into the fire. Wild burst of demoniacal music. A huge green serpent with movable jaw rises from flame behind the altar and strikes viciously at HERZOG. The raven croaks, flaps its wings, and shows its illuminated eyes. The leaves of the adder plant open and disclose demons and serpents as before. Skeleton forms appear above on rocks, pointing to HERZOG. Music changes to tremolo piano. The adder plant remains open during the remainder of the scene.)* By the venom tongue that stills Poisoned slander till it kills. *(Casts green ingredient into the fire. Wild blasts of demoniacal music and same action as before. Music changing to tremolo piano.)* By the thief with skulking tread, Who breaks the grave and robs the dead. *(Casts blue ingredient into flame. Wild blast and same business as before.)* By all the crimes men hate and fear, Zamiel, master, now appear. *(Casts red ingredient into the fire.)* Zamiel, appear, appear!

> *(Wild blast and same business as before, in addition to which loud crashing thunder and vivid lightning, the latter showing in luminous forks in backing. Huge serpents writhe to and fro across the stage. ZAMIEL, bearing a sceptre around which is twined a green serpent, suddenly appears from stump of blasted tree, with strong light from calcium thrown upon him. He holds the picture a moment before speaking. HERZOG kneeling down. Music stops.)*

ZAMIEL. Arise! *(HERZOG rises.)* Why am I summoned?

HERZOG. My life is waning. Give me to live, feed the still currents of my sluggish veins, give me fresh charms and potencies.

ZAMIEL. Wherefore?

HERZOG. Men hate and did they not fear—would despise me. I would repay their hate with hate. I would live on, on, and in that life rival thy dread power of evil.

ZAMIEL. What wilt thou give for such a boon?

HERZOG. Whate'er thou wilt; give me but life and all I have is thine.

ZAMIEL. 'Tis not enough. What's thine is mine already.

HERZOG. What else?

ZAMIEL. Listen. A soul younger, fresher, whiter than thine, must on each recurring year be, by your arts, turned to my account.

HERZOG. I hear, dread master, and will pay the price.

ZAMIEL. For every soul thus lost to good and gained to me a year's new life is thine. A single soul, a single year, a hundred souls, a hundred years. 'Tis with thyself to live forever.

HERZOG. Forever?

ZAMIEL. Forever! But should the stroke of midnight fall a twelve-month hence and no lost soul, by you betrayed within that time, come wailing at my gates—perdition closes on your dark career. It's a compact?

HERZOG. It is.

> (*Music. ZAMIEL waves his sceptre. Thunder and lightning. A Fiend, red glare, rises through trap left, bearing a large red book, pen and inkhorn.*)

ZAMIEL. *(Pointing to book.)* Sign!

> (*Music. Thunder and lightning. Sheeted Spectres rises through trap at back and appear at left and right from behind rocks. SKULDAWELPP reappears, demons and skeletons appear from right and left, all pointing at HERZOG who takes the pen and dips it in the horn. The pen ignites and flames blue. He writes in the book, during which the raven croaks flaps its wings, etc. SERPENTS*

writhe and demoniacal laughter is heard outside and above. After he has signed ZAMIEL waves his sceptre, gong sounds and red glare descends with book, etc., amid red fire. Music stops.)

ZAMIEL. 'Tis well. Listen, slave. Within a dungeon of the eastern wing of gray and gloomy Wolfenstein there lies in chains a youth called Rodolphe. His fortunes desperate, and desperate souls, like drowning men, will catch at straws. Begin with him.

HERZOG. Dread power, I hear thy mandate and thy will obey.

(Bows low before ZAMIEL. Music. Thunder and lightning and all the action as before. Red fire from behind altar and at the wings. Red glare reappears, pointing to HERZOG. Winged serpents appear above and fiery dragon enters left, simultaneously with which GREPPO very white with hair on end rushes on right as if to communicate something.)

GREPPO. Master, I—

(He is appalled at the sight before him, utters a loud cry, falls upon his knees, clasping his hands and moving his lips as if in prayer.)

Quick Curtain

Act Two

Scene 1

A subterranean vault beneath the castle of Wolfenstein.

Set floor right. Movable in upper part of right flat. Sliding stone panel in lower part of left flat.

WULFGAR discovered chaining RODOLPHE to wall. Music at rise of curtain. Lights half down.

WULFGAR. There my fine fellow. I think you're both safe and comfortable. No entreaties; neither light nor sound ever comes here.

RODOLPHE. Wretch.

WULFGAR. When you want exercise or change of air and you can manage to get out of yonder little encumbrances—*(pointing to chains)*—you can take it in the vault beneath. Yonder trap leads to it. You may find it a little moldy, and may stumble over the skeleton of the last lodger, but that's nothing. Any change is better than no change at all.

RODOLPHE. Monster, begone.

WULFGAR. *(Taking up lamp.)* Oh certainly, anything to oblige. In the meantime, if your exercise should give you an appetite and you should want food, cry out for it. Cry loud and I won't come. Ha, ha, ha. Goodnight.

(He exits right door. Lights down.)

RODOLPHE. Alone. So ends in darkness and in death all my bright dreams of the future and must I perish thus--I who have but entered the portal of life? No, no, it cannot be! I must, I will burst these bonds. *(Music. He makes an effort to break the chains.)* 'Tis vain, they defy even the strength of despair. *(Shuddering.)* How awful is the chill of this noxious vault. It's very vapors press upon my brow like the hand of death and freeze my very marrow. *(Music. HERTZOG enters with dark lantern through sliding panel. Starting.)* Who's there?

HERTZOG. Thy friend.

RODOLPHE. Who are you?

HERTZOG. *(Turning light upon himself.)* Behold!

(Chord.)

RODOLPHE. *(Starting.)* Hertzog, the Crook!

HERTZOG. Aye, so men call me.

(Puts lantern off left.)

RODOLPHE. Ill-omened bird, what brings you here? Yet why should I ask? You come the minister of death? 'Tis well, 'tis merciful. Begin your work.

HERTZOG. Out, foolish boy. I serve no human master.

RODOLPHE. Then why are you here?

HERTZOG. I come to give thee liberty.

RODOLPHE. Liberty!

HERTZOG. Aye. Listen. I hate thine enemy. Thou lov'st a maid of whom thou hast been robbed; would'st win her back? I have the power to serve thee.

RODOLPHE. Begone, tempter. I know your power and can guess from whence it comes. Men say you deal in dark and necromantic spells that warp the senses and enthrall the soul.

HERTZOG. Pah! Art thou, too, tainted with the vulgar fear that calls philosophy-the natural working of great Nature's laws- a spell of darkness? It is the light, weak boy, the light, which we sage men, who waste our lives oe'r midnight lamps, glean from dull vapors for the sluggards' use. Fools sneer the most when least they understand and brand as foul what Nature stamps as fair. Thy gains gall thee, let me loose them.

(He touches them with his staff. They fall to ground.)

RODOLPHE. *(Coming forward.)* What is your purpose?

HERTZOG. Again I say to serve thee.

RODOLPHE. How?

HERTZOG. Listen, I will tell thee a secret. She whom thou lovest is of noble birth.

RODOLPHE. Amina?

HERTZOG. Aye, yet not Amina, but the only child and heiress of the noble house of Wellenstein, stolen when but an infant by a revengeful gypsy whom her father scourged and given to gabbling Barbara.

RODOLPHE. Amina noble?

HERTZOG. Aye, and thou of humble birth, but gold can buy nobility—nay more, can give thee power to cross thine enemy.

RODOLPHE. Why talk to me of gold-to me, the poorest of the poor, whose purse contains not half so much as one poor silver mark.

HERTZOG. Thou'rt poor indeed, but thou art poor because thou wilt be poor. 'Tis with thyself to shame the wealth of the mighty Croesus.

RODOLPHE. How?

HERTZOG. Hast thou not heard of glittering gold in massive piles fast locked within these mountains?

RODOLPHE. An idle tale, a senseless fable told by crooning gossips. A treasure often sought but never found and some do say 'tis death to seek it.

HERTZOG. I tell thee, boy, the story's true, this gold is palpable to sight and touch, and may be garnered too, if thou art bold enough.

RODOLPHE. I'll hear no more! Thou'dst take advantage of my desperate strait to work some juggle to entrap my soul. Begone I say, begone!

HERTZOG. And leave thee to thy doom?

RODOLPHE. Aye.

HERTZOG. And thy affianced bride—would'st thou so like a graven yield her up onto thine enemy?

RODOLPHE. Oh, agony!

HERTZOG. 'Tis true she loves thee, but bethink thee, boy, she is but woman and she may be won. Her noble birth is known to Wolfenstein who means to wed her, and with her fortune to prop his falling house. Already flattered by his serpent tongue, she dries her tears and listens to his suit.

RODOLPHE. 'Tis false!

HERTZOG. 'Tis true!

RODOLPHE. The proof?

HERTZOG. Behold.

(Music. He waves his staff. Panel in upper part of flat slides open, showing through gauze WOLFENSTEIN and AMINA, the former clasping the hand and kneeling at the feet of the latter whose face is averted. Picture strongly lighted.)

RODOLPHE. *(Starting forward.)* By Heaven, he shall not!

HERTZOG. *(Interposing; waves his staff; panel closes.)* Bravely said! Bravely said!

RODOLPHE. *(Turning quickly.)* What dev'lish compact would you have me sign? Propose it while my reason whirls and desperation aids your dam'd design. If by the act I snatch her from his grasp, I'll pay the ransom though it reach my soul. *(HERTZOG with face averted chuckles sardonically.)* Come, philosopher or fiend, whate'er thou art; the price, I say, the price.

HERTZOG. Pah! I ask no compact. I would serve thee gratis. I but demand that thou shalt serve thyself. Be rich and thou'lt be powerful. In thy revenge upon thine enemy and mine, thou'lt pay thy debt to me with interest.

RODOLPHE. Where lies this wondrous treasure?

HERTZOG. Listen. Amid the fastnesses of the Hartz beyond the outlet of the Black Gorge lies a small lake whose waters few have ever gazed upon, for vulgar fear and superstitious dread have long since marked it for enchanted ground.

RODOLPHE. I've heard the story.

HERTZOG. Trace carefully its northern shore until a rock rising like a wall bars further passage beneath a fringe of tangled vines you'll find a boat concealed. Behold this talisman ring! *(Takes a large ring from his finger.)* 'Tis a magnet of wondrous power. When thou hast found the boat step boldly in. This ring will guide thee safely to the entrance of the golden cavern within the compass of whose glittering walls thy wondering eyes may feast on wealth far greater than the coffers of the world can boast.

RODOLPHE. Give me the ring.

HERTZOG. 'Tis thine. *(Gives ring.)* Stay, thou'lt need a henchman. *(Stamps his foot.)* Varlet, come forth. *(Music. Panel on flat opens as before and GREPPO enters. Aside:)* He too shall perish.

GREPPO. Your will, Master?

HERTZOG. To part with three.

GREPPO. *(Aside.)* Oh, if this should be true. *(Aloud.)* With me?

HERTZOG. With thee, knave.

GREPPO. Wherefore?

HERTZOG. I weary with thine appetite.

GREPPO. *(Aside.)* Here's a chance. Oh here is a chance if he but stick to it. I must seem unwilling lest he repent. *(Aloud.)* Dear master, I will reform, believe me, I will reform. Allowance me to what would starve a mouse. Nay more, to pleasure you, I will not eat at all. I'll live on air, but do not cast me off.

HERTZOG. I am resolved. Behold thy future master. *(To RODOLPHE.)* Thou'lt find him faithful but he breeds a famine. Take for the present need this purse of gold. *(Offers purse; RODOLPHE by a gesture refuses it.)* Nay, when thou'rt rich thou canst repay it.

RODOLPHE. *(Taking purse.)* Nay, more, if what you say be true, eternal gratitude—

HERTZOG. Pah, you trifle time. *(Moves staff; panel opens.)* Yonder lies your path; it is a glorious one. Begone.

RODOLPHE. Farewell. Come, boy, come.

(Music. He exits at panel. GREPPO, following turns to entreat HERTZOG, who raises his staff threateningly. GREPPO exits hurriedly at panel.)

HERTZOG. *(Stands in opening and chuckling gazes after them.)* The thought of vengeance stirs within his heart; the lust of gold is rising in his soul, the path that leads to where 'tis hoarded ends in death. He's mine, ha, ha! He's mine.

Curtain

Act Two

Scene 2

A lobby in the castle of Wolfenstein.

Enter BARBARA RH, followed by CARLINE.

BARBARA. Don't talk to me, girl. Remember your station and consider mine. Who am I and what am I that I should be lodged in a wing of the castle overlooking the dog kennels.

CARLINE. Your ladyship is quite right to revel and when I advised your ladyship to calm yourself it was out of consideration for your ladyship's eyes. Any little flurry does so spoil the natural beauty of their expression.

BARBARA. Carline, you're a good girl, you're a considerate girl and I forgive you, but eyes or no eyes, I'll not be imposed upon. Where's Mynheer Von Puffengruntz? Where's his lordship's chamberlain?

CARLINE. *(Looking left.)* Here he comes down the great stairway as full of flesh and scant of breath as ever. *(Aside.)* And as the waddling old porpoise appears to have a liquorice tooth for this silly old buzzard I'll leave them to bill and coo while I run off to comfort dear 'Mina who has passed the whole night in tears for poor Rodolphe.

(VON PUFF enters. CARLINE curtseys and exits.)

VON PUFF. Eh, what! Madam Barbara, stirring so early! Why, bless my soul, the mist of the mountain is yet hanging upon the turrets of the castle.

BARBARA. Then let it hang and be hanged to it. Stirring indeed! Haven't I been stirring all night and wouldn't the seven sleepers have been stirring all night too, if they had lodged where I did?

VON PUFF. Surely nothing has had the audacity to disturb the quiet of your chamber?

BARBARA. Nothing? To begin with, do you call such a storm as that of last night nothing? Why the thunder crashed over the castle loud enough to wake the dead. That was bad enough, but only to think that I, the right honorable foster mother that is to be to her right honorable ladyship that is to be passing the night in apartments overlooking a dog-kennel.

VON PUFF. A dog-kennel?

BARBARA. Aye, a kennel of great, savage hounds, fed late at night on raw meat on purpose to give them the nightmare and make them dream all night long of chasing wild boars in the forest. Ugh! I shall never get their terrible yelping out of my head.

VON PUFF. Believe me, my dear Madam Barbara, it is the first time the brutes ever were known to have been unruly. I promise that they shall be soundly punished and instantly removed. But I too am criminal. The apartments were selected by me because they command the best view of the mountains.

BARBARA. But I don't want to look at the mountains. I got a glimpse of it from one of the north windows last night during the storm and it looked for all the world like Beelzebub and his imps were holding a jubilee there.

VON PUFF. Enough, my dear Madam Barbara, enough. If the mountain is unpleasant, it shall be removed. No, no! I mean you shall be removed. *(Approaching her in a wheedling manner.)* Will it please you to accompany me and choose for yourself?

BARBARA. *(Simperingly.)* Really, Mynheer Von Puffengruntz, you have such mollifying ways that—that—

VON PUFF. *(Taking her hand.)* Oh-o-o.

BARBARA. Would it be prudent? Dare I trust myself? We poor silly things are so weak and you mean so naughty that—that—

(Leans her head upon his shoulder, looks up into his face and sighs.)

VON PUFF. Confiding innocence, rely upon the honor of a Von Puffengruntz.

(Looks around, sighs, kisses her. BARBARA utters a faint scream and hiding her face in her fan is led offstage by VON PUFF chuckling.)

Curtain

Act Two

Scene 3

A wild pass in the Hartz mountains.

Music. Lights down. Enter RODOLPHE and GREPPO, each bearing an Alpine staff. GREPPO in improved condition.

RODOLPHE. A strange weird place and one it seems not often tried by human footsteps. I fear we've missed the way. What think you, Master Greppo?

GREPPO. *(Aside.)* Master Greppo! Master Greppo! He calls me Master Greppo! Here's an honor and here's a master. Oh such a master, such a liberal master as this stuffed belly, tight as any drum with goodly provender and generous wine will testify. *(To RODOLPHE.)* What think I, princely master?

RODOLPHE. Aye.

GREPPO. Why since you honor me with consultation and give me leave to think at all—a privilege grown rusty from great lack of use—I say we're right and that the lake we seek is near at hand.

RODOLPHE. Why think you so?

GREPPO. Because just now I heard a bittern cry and twice ere that I heard a marsh-frog croak, and as they're both accounted water-fowl, 'twere safe to say that we're near the water.

RODOLPHE. Then lead us on. *(Crossing left.)* Ere long the rising moon will pierce this veil of mist and light us to our golden haven. Come.

(He exits left.)

GREPPO. I follow

(He exits. Change very slowly—no whistle.)

Curtain

Act Two

Scene 4

The grotto of golden stalactites.

A grand and comprehensive water cavern of gold, deeply perspective, with stalactiform arched roof. Cut wings, representing vistas, running parallel and harmonizing with that of the main grotto, the mouth of which (5 feet high by 5 feet wide) discloses an open lake and distant shore at back. Set transparent silver waters, in which are seen sporting fishes and nondescript amphibian; diminutive fairies asleep on the waters of the grotto in golden shells. Set ground or shore-piece, richly studded with gold and jewels. Set masses of emerald and gold, upon and at the foot of which are reclining gnomes and amphibian. FAIRIES asleep in poses. The Moon, seen through the opening at the back

The Black Crook

and over the distant shore of the lake, shows red upon its face at the opening of the scene. Music. Shortly afterward, DRAGONFIN, who has been asleep on a jewelled mass on the shore, slowly awakens, rises and stretches himself. Upon turning he sees the red upon the face of the moon. Music.

DRAGONFIN. *(Uttering a cry of alarm.)* Awake, awake! *(Music hurried. GNOMES and AMPHIBEA spring to their feet; fairies and water nymphs enter hurriedly, diminutive fairies in shells and fairies poses awaken.)* Behold there's blood upon the face of the moon. Our queen's in danger. To arms! To arms! *(MUSIC hurried. The sprites in the shells disappear. The GNOMES, AMPHIBEA and FAIRIES rush off and immediately re-enter armed. The first named with knotted clubs and tridents, the Fairies with javelins. During the action the red disappears from the face of the moon and it resumes its natural color. Seeing the change.)* Stay, 'tis past. Hark. *(STALACTA is heard singing beneath the waters. ALL bend forward and listen. After song:)* 'Tis she, our queen.

(ALL kneel. Music. STALACTA rises from the water and steps on shore, assisted by DRAGONFIN.)

STALACTA. Arise, my loving subjects.

(ALL rise.)

DRAGONFIN. Mistress, but now the light in yon great sapphire died out and stains of blood flushed in the face of the pale moon. You have escaped some deadly peril.

STALACTA. You are right. Listen all. Tonight while wandering in the fastnesses of the Hartz without my protecting talisman, I heedlessly trod within one of the charmed circles of our enemy, the arch fiend Zamiel.

ALL. Ha!

STALACTA. On the instant I was transformed into a white dove with shorn pinions. From beneath the rank leaves of an adder-plant glided a huge serpent. Its eyes were burning coals, its tongue a living flame. I was paralyzed with fear and powerless to move. Nearer and nearer it came. I felt its stifling breath displace the purer air. I saw its venom fangs glist'ning in the pale moonlight. Rising from out its deadly coil itself, when suddenly a youth, a mortal, strangely present in that wildwood spot, seeing the danger of the trembling bird seized a dead bough, which chance had fashioned like a holy cross, and smote the foul thing dead. Then bore me safely from the charmed spot and gave me life and liberty.

DRAGONFIN. Revenge, revenge on the minions of Zamiel.

(He goes quickly off right.)

ALL. Revenge, revenge!

STALACTA. Nay, let no thought other than of joy mingle with this happy time. Remember, 'tis my natal hour, and I would have it, as in the past, a festal one. Let the invisible harmonies of this our realm breathe sweetest concord only. And you, bright Crystalline, with your four sisters, chase with flying feet the silver hours.

> *(Seats herself on bank center. Music. The fairies form for dance. After the first pose a loud prolonged warning note, as if from a shell is heard outside at back. all start in alarm and those hold the attitude of listening. The sound is repeated. Music hurried. The pose is broken and the FAIRIES, GNOMES, and AMPHIBEA the latter seizing their arms form an alarm on either side. DRAGONFIN appears quickly through trap and lands in front of ground piece. STALACTA at the first sound springs to her feet.)*

STALACTA. Speak, what danger threatens?

DRAGONFIN. The sentinel shells, played upon by the watchful winds, give alarm. Two daring mortals, armed with the enchanted magnet of the Black Crook approach the secret entrance. Already they have passed the white whirlpool in safety. They come to despoil our realm of its glittering wealth.

STALACTA. Fear not the talisman they bear is powerless against the spells that guard the portal.

ALL. Ho, ho, ho! *(Echoed without and above. Music. Chorus by GNOMES, AMPHIBEA and FAIRIES.)*
Rejoice, rejoice, rejoice!
Sprites of the golden realm, rejoice.
Daring mortals mock our power,
Flushed with the drink that the heart makes bold,
Drunk with the thirst for the glittering gold,

They madly rush on the fatal hour.
Darks spells arise; smite their longing eyes
That they never may gaze on the glittering prize.
Rejoice, rejoice, rejoice!
Sprites of the golden realms rejoice!

STALACTA. My faithful subjects, your Queen commends the zeal with which you would guard from mortal light our beautiful realm. But ere these rash intruders perish I would gratify a strange desire. Speed hence good Dragonfin. Catch me their shadows from the bosom of the moon-lighted lake and cast them upon my faithful mirror. I would look upon them ere they fade forever. *(Music. DRAGONFIN prostrates himself before STALACTA, springs into the water and disappears.)* Begin the spell.

(Music.)

CHORUS BY FAIRIES.
Mortal shadows dimly cast
By the moonbeam's mystic ray
In the bosom of the lake
Hither, hither fly away,
Flitting through the silver sheen
Come at summons of our Queen.
Guardian spirits let them pass;
Cast their shadows on the glass.

(Music. DRAGONFIN springs from the water, and after prostrating himself before the QUEEN, rises and points to the water. FAIRIES wave their wands. A small arched headed frame of gold and coral stalactites rises center at the distant entrance of the grotto, showing small figures of Rodolphe and Greppo in boat, the former at the prow gazing anxiously forward, the latter aft in the attitude of paddling. STALACTA who had crossed down right turns when the picture is fully shown. Chord. Starting.)

STALACTA. Ha, 'tis he! He must not perish. Invisible spirits, avert this peril. Shades of mortals hovering near, join your masters; disappear. *(Music, hurry. The mirror and figures quickly sink)* Dragonfin, come hither. Fly with swiftest speed to the rock beneath the waters of the guarded entrance. When the frail bark which now approaches shall be rent asunder by the relentless spells that guard our realm, be at your task to snatch from death these daring mortals and bear them safely hither.

ALL. *(Starting forward inquiringly.)* Mistress!

STALACTA. Nay, question me not, away, away. Slaves of my power, obey, obey.

> *(Music. Hurry. DRAGONFIN bows low, springs into the water and disappears. Music. A small boat with two mechanical figures or small doubles of Rodolphe and Greppo, as they appeared in the mirror, appears from left outside at the distance entrance of the cavern and moves very slowly across. When it reaches the center of the opening it sinks at the sound of the gong and flash of lightning at back. Music. Hurry. All the GNOMES, AMPHIBEA, etc. utter examinations of delight and indulge in extravagant antics, until checked by a gesture from STALACTA. Soft music. DRAGONFIN rises slowly from water, supporting on either side RODOLPHE and GREPPO, the latter gasping violently for breath as his head appears. They step on shore. RODOLPHE and GREPPO lost in bewilderment. DRAGONFIN bows low before STALACTA. The other Amphibea and Gnomes make a demonstration of attack. STALACTA steps between.)*

STALACTA. Forbear! Who moves again 'till I alone command shall perish.

> *(They retire.)*

RODOLPHE. *(Rubbing his eyes.)* Is this a phantasm—this glittering gold, yon flashing gems, these strange fantastic shapes? Have I then passed the portal of an unknown world or am I dreaming?

STALACTA. Welcome, brave mortal, to our bright domain. And you my subjects, know and greet your Queen's preserver.

> *(Music. GNOMES and AMPHIBEA cluster around RODOLPHE and GREPPO, rolling at their feet and indulging in various grateful antics, after which the fairies surround them and evince their delight.)*

RODOLPHE. *(Still bewildered.)* If this indeed be not a dream, tell me, bright being—you whose simple motion seems to sway the moods and passions of this elfin band, who art thou and where am I?

STALACTA. I am called Stalacta, queen of this dazzling realm. The glittering wonders that assail thine eyes are not creations of fantastic dreams but Nature's handiwork wrought with cunning fingers in a bounteous mood.

GREPPO. *(Who has picked up a large mass of gold at back comes forward.)* 'Tis true, master, 'tis true. Behold this shining nugget.

STALACTA. Who is thy droll companion?

RODOLPHE. My simple henchman, a faithful guide and servitor.

STALACTA. I bid him welcome for his master's sake.

GREPPO. Thanks, thanks, your resplendent majesty, thanks.

RODOLPHE. You speak of service done; have we then met before?

STALACTA. Yes, once.

RODOLPHE. Indeed! When?

STALACTA. This very night.

RODOLPHE. Tonight?

STALACTA. Tonight, in the glen of fire, but not as now. Then a poor weak, fluttering, charm-encompassed bird, you snatched me from the jaws of death, broke the dark spell of transformation and gave to me the priceless boon of liberty.

RODOLPHE. I do remember—

GREPPO. And so do I. Phew, how the sparks flew when master smashed the head of the scaly monster. And such a smell of brimstone. I do believe it was one of the Beelzebub's own imps in disguise.

STALACTA. Again thou art welcome. This is my natal hour. Wilt view the sports of this our carnival?

RODOLPHE. Most willingly.

STALACTA. And while the revels proceed thou shalt tell me thy story.

(Music. Seats are brought forward by AMPHIBEA. STALACTA and RODOLPHE sit. GREPPO disposes himself left, amusing himself with DRAGONFIN, GNOMES and

The Black Crook

AMPHIBEA, who present him from time to time with nuggets of gold and jewels which he thrusts into his pockets until they become greatly distended, during which action the diminutive sprites re-appear in shells on water floating to and from fishing. The FAIRIES form for dance. Grand ballet action by principals and full corps de ballet, during which the fishers in the shells are seen to catch some small silver fish.)

GREPPO. *(After the dance terminates.)* Ha, ha, dancing; all very well in its way, but there's the sport for me, fishing! Look, master, look; see the little rogues hook the silly shiners. Oh, if there's one thing in the world I love more than another its fishing-- such fun to feel the greedy rascals snap and see them wiggle. There's another. Oh I can't stand it any longer; fishing's like the measles, it's catching. *(Turning to AMPHIBEA and GNOMES.)* Would any of you handsome gentlemen oblige me with a spare hook and line?

(DRAGONFIN nods assent and brings him rod and line.)

GREPPO. Well, upon my word, I'm very much obliged to your scaly magnificence. I'll do as much for you someday. By the way, is your amphibious majesty fond of fish? *(DRAGONFIN nods affirmatively.)* What kind? *(DRAGONFIN indicates that he likes large ones.)* Like large ones, eh? All right, I'll make you a present of the first ten-pounder I catch.

(Music. He fishes from the shore and catches two small fishes, the last quite diminutive. The AMPHIBEA, GNOMES and FAIRIES laugh boisterously as each fish is drawn forth. GREPPO coming down crestfallen)

GREPPO. Pshaw, mere sprats and sardines. Not my kind at all. This is too much like taking advantage of confiding innocence. *(To DRAGONFIN.)* Couldn't your finny excellency oblige me with a more tempting bait, something that would seduce some big, greedy, wiggly-waggly fellow into taking a nibble?

(DRAGONFIN nods affirmatively. Music. DRAGONFIN goes to the margin of the water and draws out a large crab which he places in the hand of GREPPO. It seizes him by the finger to the great delight of the AMPHIBEA, GNOMES and FAIRIES. He struggles frantically to extricate himself and is finally released by

DRAGONFIN who baits the hook with the crab and gives him the rod and line. GREPPO takes DRAGONFIN apart confidentially.)

GREPPO. I don't know about this. Excuse me for asking the question, but, as an unprejudiced observer, don't you think this style of bait more likely to bite the fish than the fish to bite the bait? *(DRAGONFIN shakes his head and indicates a large fish will take it.)* All right, here goes then.

(Music. He casts the line into the water. A moment after it is violently seized and a frantic struggle ensures, during which he is nearly drawn overboard two or three times. Suddenly an amphibeous monster spring from the water and pursues GREPPO around, off and on the stage to the great delight of the AMPHIBEA, GNOMES and FAIRIES who indulge in boisterous laughter. GREPPO in his terror throws himself at the feet of STALACTA for protection. She rises and waves her hand. The monster retires and is pacified by DRAGONFIN. GREPPO comes forward.)

GREPPO. Really, my fishy-fleshy friend, you must excuse me. I beg ten thousand pardons. I hadn't the remotest idea in the world that any of you bottle green gentlemen were lying around loose in the bottom watching for a supper of raw crabs. Indeed I hadn't.*(The monster growls and makes a start at him. Music. DRAGONFIN interposes and pacifies the monster by putting him on the back, the taking his hand passes it into that of GREPPO. GREPPO shakes monster's hand cordially.)* All right, I accept your apology. *(Turning to DRAGONFIN.)* Now you're what I call a true friend--a friend in need. You stick by a fellow when he hasn't the courage to stick by himself. This is the second time you've done me a service. Once in saving me from too much water and now in saving me from too much luck, and I'll let you see that I can be grateful. You like fish? *(DRAGONFIN nods affirmatively. Passing the monster over to him.)* Consider him yours.

(All the AMPHIBEA, GNOMES and FAIRIES laugh and go up stage.)

STALACTA. *(Rising and leading RODOLPHE forward.)* Thy story claims for thee my pity and my aid.

RODOLPHE. And Hertzog, the Black Crook—

STALACTA. Is a vile sorcerer whose dark unhallowed spells were wrought for thy destruction.

RODOLPHE. How!

STALACTA. Beneath the entrance to this charmed spot lie intertwined among the branches of the coralline whole hecatombs of human bones, the whitened relics of adventurous mortals who like thyself have sought this realm. Until tonight no human eye has ever seen the dazzling splendor of this wondrous dome. No human footsteps save thine own and his who follows thee have ever pressed these sands of gold. Had not thy coming been to me foreshadowed and all my power been interposed to snatch thee from the impending doom, thou too had'st joined the hapless throng that moldering lies beneath yon depths.

RODOLPHE. Then is thy debt to me already paid.

STALACTA. Not so. I am still thy debtor and must ever be. Thou art environed by danger and need the power of my protection. Return into the outer world again; thy happiness is there. She whom thou lov'st is worthy of thy love; therefore return.

RODOLPHE. Amina, dear Amina!

STALACTA. In the secret cells of this cavern whose walls are solid gold lie countless hoards of richest treasure, gleaned for ages by the tireless gnomes. In the crystal depths of these waters sparkle gems richer by far than human eyes have ever gazed upon. Of these thou shalt bear with thee the choicest. Behold my gift. *(Music. A jewelled stalactiform etagere with strong light from calcium on it rises center in front of ground-piece bearing upon its different shelves rich vases filled with gold and various colored jewels which DRAGONFIN, GNOMES and AMPHIBEA remove, performing a series of grotesque evolutions to marked Music. Etagere sinks—after which music. STALACTA waves her hand; a golden boat studded with jewels glides on from right.)* This bark, protected by a potent spell shall bear thee safely to yon neighboring shore. My faithful gnomes shall be the treasure bearers. But ere we part, take thou this jewelled circlet. *(Gives him a ring from her finger.)* Should danger threaten as perchance it will, for baffled malice has a thousand stings—press but thy lips upon the gem and thou wilt find me by thy side. *(Music. RODOLPHE kneels and kisses her hand. Raising him.)* Farewell.

> *(Music. RODOLPHE steps into the boat. GREPPO, bearing a large mass of gold affectionately embraces DRAGONFIN, shakes hands with the GNOMES and AMPHIBEA, kisses the fairies, bows low to STALACTA and gets into the boat. A dolphin, glittering in green and gold, rises from behind waters with principal danseuse bearing vase of treasure. Other dolphins float on with diminutive sprites bearing treasure. Copious shower of gold, the other sprites on the water catching the flakes in silver shells. Roses by GNOMES, AMPHIBEA and FAIRIES. The whole scene brilliantly lighted.)*

Slow Curtain

Act Three

Scene 1

Illuminated gardens of Wolfenstein.

Six Months later. Moonlight with terrace and illuminated castle at back. This scene, standing as it does, the entire act, should be elaborate and beautiful.

Music at rise. Masqueraders in ball costume discovered promenading. Grand Ballet divertissement, after which the masquers gradually disappear at different entrances. Enter from the terrace BARBARA, masked, flauntingly dressed and carrying a huge fan, followed by CARLINE.

BARBARA. *(Unmasking and coming forward.)* Phew, what a relief. Thank the saints his Countship's birthday comes but once a year. Another such festival would be the death of me. Ah! I'm stewed, fried, boiled and roasted.

> *(Fans herself vigorously.)*

CARLINE. *(Aside.)* And still as tough as Dame Gretchen's gander that was twenty-one last Easter. *(Aloud.)* Why, Madame Barbara, I thought you enjoyed it.

BARBARA. So I do, child, so I do, particularly the masquerading. One has so many pleasant things whispered in one's ear, but I can't say much for the waltzing. It's such a terrible thing to take the starch out of one's linen.

CARLINE. Madame Barbara, what's a little starch? Nothing. If I waltzed as gracefully as you—*(BARBARA makes a gesture of satisfaction)*—and has such an inviting waist—*(BARBARA pinches her waist)*—I'd keep at it until I was as limp as a boiled cabbage leaf.

BARBARA. Then you—you think me graceful, eh?

CARLINE. *(Aside.)* As a hippopotamus. *(Aloud.)* As a sylph. You were the envy of all the ladies and the admiration of all the other sex. Did you notice the courtly gentleman in the blue mask?

BARBARA. He who danced so often with the lady Amina?

CARLINE. Yes, Madame.

BARBARA. And what of him?

CARLINE. Nothing, only he was frantic to get an introduction to you.

BARBARA. No was he?

CARLINE. Yes indeed, Madame. And when his lordship the count engaged the lady Amina for a moment, he turned to me, and slipping a golden crown into my palm with one hand, pressing his heart with the other, asked with a sweet sighing silvery voice, trembling with emotion, "Who is that lovely being?"

BARBARA. No! Did he?

CARLINE. Yes indeed, Madame. *(Aside.)* The saints forgive me for lying. *(Aloud.)* And Mynheer Von Puffengruntz, who overheard him, turned pea-green with jealousy.

BARBARA. *(Fanning herself and pressing her hand upon her heart.)* Be still, little trembler, be still. I declare, my silly heart is fluttering like a poor little starling in a gold cage.

CARLINE. *(Aside.)* More like a big buzzard in a steel trap.

BARBARA. Carline, take my fan, child. *(Gives it.)* The exertion will make my complexion too ruddy.

CARLINE. So it will, Madame, and ruddy complexions are not genteel. Allow me.

(Fans her vigorously)

BARBARA. Not so violent, girl. You'll disarrange my hair. Gently, very gently, a sort of sportive zephyr.

CARLINE. I understand, Madame. You want a mild sort of tickling sensation-- something like one feels on one's neck when a gentleman whispers in one's ear.

BARBARA. *(Languidly.)* Ye-es. *(Sighs.)* And he called me a—a—what did he call me?

CARLINE. A swan-like creature. *(Aside.)* A goose.

BARBARA. Oh. *(Sighs.)* Who can he be, I wonder.

CARLINE. Nobody appears to know exactly, I heard his lordship the Count whisper to the Baron von Puffengruntz that he suspected the mysterious blue mask to be no other than the young prince Leopold. Once, while dancing, his domino came open at the breast and I saw a collar of jewels fit for an Emperor. However, as everybody is to unmask at the grand banquet, we will then know all about him.

BARBARA. Eh, what, the Prince Leopold?

CARLINE. So his lordship the Count thinks.

BARBARA. Why he's already affianced as everybody knows, to the young Princess Frederica.

CARLINE. Dear me, so he is. How unfortunate!

BARBARA. Poor young man, how I pity him. What a terrible thing it is to be of royal blood and not have the liberty to choose for one's self. Heigh-ho! I know it is a sad, cruel, wicked thing to blight a young and budding affection, but as the right honorable foster-mother that is to be of her right honorable ladyship that is to be, I mustn't encourage his highness in a hopeless passion.

(Displays herself.)

VON PUFF. *(Entering from terrace and stands at back, admiringly.)* There she is! What a grace. What a dignity. What a walk. *(Coming forward.)* Ah-a-a!

BARBARA. *(Sighing.)* There's another victim to love's cruel dart. My fan, child.

CARLINE. *(Giving it.)* Be careful, use it gently Madame. Remember your complexion. *(Aside.)* What a lovely couple—powder and puff.

VON PUFF. *(Aside.)* What a golden opportunity. *(Aloud.)* Young woman, as I left the grand hall I heard your mistress asking for you.

CARLINE. *(Aside.)* Of course, I understand, cunning old walrus. May I retire, Madame?

BARBARA. Yes, certainly child, that is if her ladyship requires you.

(Coquettes with her dress, etc.)

CARLINE. *(Aside.)* I thought so, willing old pelican. She's beginning to preen her feathers already. Never mind, I shall have another flirtation with the prince's equerry, the drollest and most agreeable fellow in the world, and such a rogue.

(Exit terrace left. VON PUFF gazes admiringly at BARBARA and sighs.)

BARBARA. *(Casting sidelong glances at him.)* Heigh-ho! There he is. My charms tonight have completed the conquest. He's fast bound in the bonds of rosy cupid. I see a proposal in one eye and a marriage settlement in the other, but I mustn't draw him in too suddenly. These men are like trout, they must be played with a little.

VON PUFF. Full moon of the festival, why have you so cruelly robbed the grand hall of your light, and left us to grope about in the dull glimmer of the sickly stars.

BARBARA. Don't talk to me about moonship and sickly stars, you heartless, gay deceiver.

VON PUFF. Deceiver!

BARBARA. Deceiver. Didn't I see you gallivanting with the Fraulein Von Skragneck, the new Burgonmaster's daughter?

VON PUFF. Politeness, my dear Madame Barbara, merely politeness, on my honor. The fact is I—I had the misfortune to tread on the lady's favorite bunion, and what you mistook for tenderness was only an apology—an apology, believe me, my dear Madame Barbara, only an apology.

BARBARA. Oh, you men, you deceiving men, you are always ready with an excuse.

VON PUFF. On the honor of a Von Puffengruntz, I swear I speak the truth. The Fraulein Von Skragneck indeed! Haven't I got eyes? Ah, cruel fair one, compared with her and all others, you are the stately sunflower in a meadow of dandelions. As—as—as the queen hollyhock in a garden of chickweed.

(Music. Tremelo piano. DRAGONFIN ascends quickly through trap. He steps forward and listens.)

BARBARA. It's coming at last, I know it's coming. *(Pressing her heart.)* What a strange flutter. I hope I'm not going to faint. Dear me, what weak silly creatures we are. I must nerve myself for the trying occasion. How fortunate it is that I happen to have my smelling salts about me.

(Draws flask from his pocket, turns back to VON PUFF and drinks.)

VON PUFF. She's moved. She's overcome with emotion, she turns to hide her blushes. She yields, and now, like a conqueror, I'll gather in the fruits of victory. *(He kneels with difficulty at the feet of BARBARA, his face half-averted, and is about to take her hand when DRAGONFIN glides quietly back of and between them, extends his left hand to VON PUFF and takes BARBARA'S in the other. Both sigh. Squeezing the hand of DRAGONFIN who shakes with suppressed laughter.)* Poor, frightened thing, how she trembles.

BARBARA. Dear me, how strangely the tender passion affects him. He's shaking like an aspen and his hand is as cold as ice.

VON PUFF. Bewitching siren, listen to the voice of love.

BARBARA. Oh, Mynheer Von Puffengruntz, how can you—

VON PUFF. Don't call me Von Puffengruntz, call be Maximillian, call me your Maximillian.

(Squeezes DRAGONFIN'S hand; DRAGONFIN squeezes BARBARA'S.)

BARBARA. Oh, don't, you naughty man, you—you hurt my hand.

VON PUFF. No, did I? Queen of love and beauty, then let me heal the bruise. *(Kisses the hand of DRAGONFIN rapturously who, at the same time, kisses BARBARA'S.)* And now that I've healed it let me call it mine.

(Looks for the first time attentively at the hand, continues inspection up the arm until he encounters the grinning face of DRAGONFIN, when in speechless terror he drops the hand, makes various floundering attempts to regain his feet and exits hurriedly.)

BARBARA. *(Aside.)* Shall I keep him a little longer with Cupid's dart sticking in his bosom, or shall I end his misery. *(Aloud.)* Ahem, you'll-you'll never be a haughty boy again? *(DRAGONFIN squeezes her hand.)* And you'll promise never to tread on the Froulein von Skragneck's bunion? *(DRAGONFIN squeezes her hand. Aside.)* Poor fellow, joy has made him speechless; he can only answer with a squeeze of the hand. *(Aloud.)* Well then, Maximillian, I'm yours.

(Falls into DRAGONFINS'S arms, looks up into his face. Music. She utters a piercing scream and rushes off stage. DRAGONFIN imitates and indulges in extravagant antics until music changes, when he starts, inclines his ear to the ground and listens—rises, moves cautiously to right, starts, pointing off right, shakes his clenched hand threateningly and quickly disappears through trap.)

HERTZOG. *(Entering hurriedly and disturbed.)* Foiled, tricked, crossed in the hour of my victory. A life desperately played for and fairly won snatched from the jaws of death. He lives, my chosen victim lives, and flushed with triumph and vast hoards of gold, stalks boldly forth to mock. Oh curse the interposing power the stepped between us. A withering palsy light upon her arm and blight and pestilence infect the air she breathes! Oh impotent, on, driveling fool. To work, to work. A soul once tampered with must be pursued, not cast aside to tempt another. So runs the bond to which I've sealed. 'Tis well, 'tis well. I'll track him as the sleuth hound tracks the stag. He must be, shall be mine.

The Black Crook

(Music. HERTZOG exits hurriedly. Music. Re-enter MASQUERS back; they cross and disappear. Enter from terrace CARLINE, laughing immoderately, followed by GREPPO, who is dressed in a smart livery.)

CARLINE. No, no, Master Equerry, that won't do. You are very clever, very droll and you tell very funny stories, but that last joke is a trifle too much.

GREPPO. But my dear Susetta—

CARLINE. *(Laughing.)* There, there. I knew you were not in earnest. My name's not Susetta.

GREPPO. Of course it isn't. It's—it's—what is it?

CARLINE. No it isn't "what is it." It's Carline.

GREPPO. Of course it is, but you see I always mean Carline when I say Susetta. Therefore Susetta-that is my dear Carline, when I tell you I love you—

CARLINE. *(Laughing.)* I don't believe a word you say. Why you arrived here scarcely three hours ago, and you've already been making love to half the girls in the castle.

GREPPO. It's a mistake, my dear Susetta—I mean Carline, altogether a mistake. I had my eye on you from the first, and any little outside pleasantry you may have happened to notice was only to get my hand in.

CARLINE. And this is only to keep it in, I suppose. No, no. I'm not as simple as I look, and I tell you, clever master Equerry, it won't do.

GREPPO. But my dear Carline, allow me to tell you that I'm not an equerry.

CARLINE. No?

GREPPO. *(Drawing himself up.)* I'm consulting secretary, confidential adviser, portable treasury, and principal disbursing officer to his highness the Prince. *(Aside.)* Everybody takes matter for a Prince and it's no part of my business to undeceive them. Besides if he isn't a Prince he deserves to be and I ought to be his Prime Minister.

CARLINE. Dear me! Consulting Secretary?

GREPPO. Consulting Secretary!

CARLINE. Confidential Adviser?

GREPPO. Confidential Adviser!

CARLINE. Portable Treasury!

GREPPO. Portable Treasury. Behold! *(Showing two glittering purses.)* Here are two purses, my master's and my own. From this— *(showing one nearly empty)*—by the Prince's order came the gold I scattered among the servants in the courtyard. With this— *(showing full one)*—I intend to endow the maiden of my choice.

CARLINE. And you really mean—

GREPPO. That you are she.

CARLINE. No.

GREPPO. Yes.

CARLINE. I'm afraid to trust you.

GREPPO. Allow me to make a deposit.

(He gives over the purse.)

CARLINE. *(Opening and admiring purse.)* Oh, dear, you've taken my breath away.

GREPPO. No, have I? Permit me to return it to you. *(Kisses her.)* Now listen, my dear little Carline, I have a secret and as there should be no secrets between man and wife--that is, man and wife that are to be, I'm going to share it with you.

CARLINE. A secret, dear Greppo?

GREPPO. Dear Greppo! Oh, say that again.

CARLINE. *(With increased tenderness.)* Well then, dear Greppo.

GREPPO. Oh, thank you. You needn't repeat it again at present. That's as much as I can stand 'till I get used to it.

CARLINE. Well, then, the secret.

GREPPO. Yes. In the first place, do you love your mistress, Carline?

CARLINE. Love her? I'd die for her.

GREPPO. No, no, no, no. I don't want you to go quite that far. I'm not ambitious to be a widower before I've had my honeymoon.

CARLINE. Well, then, I love her dearly.

GREPPO. That's better. And she loves my mas—that is, young Rodolphe the painter?

CARLINE. Better than her own life, poor lady.

GREPPO. And would marry him but for this ruffian Count Wolfenstein?

CARLINE. Yes—but the secret.

GREPPO. *(With caution.)* Well, then, you must know—*(Music.)* Hark, somebody's coming.

> *(Enter from terrace RODOLPHE and AMINA. He is brilliantly dressed, wearing a collar and other ornaments of glittering jewels, blue mask and domino. AMINA also wears mask and domino.)*

AMINA. Some one is here.

RODOLPHE. Fear not; they are our own people. *(Comes forward with AMINA.)* Leave us, good Greppo, and take your companion with you.

GREPPO. Yes, good master. Come along, Carline.

CARLINE. Surely I've heard that voice before?

GREPPO. *(Taking her arm.)* Hush. That's the secret I was going to share with you, and if you'll take a stroll with me in the ramble that leads to the lover's paradise I'll tell you all about it.

CARLINE. Yes, dear Greppo.

GREPPO. Oh, don't!

> *(Music. They go off left. RODOLPHE and AMINA unmask.)*

AMINA. Oh, dear Rodolphe, is this a dream?

RODOLPHE. What's past seems so, but day has dawned on our long clouded night and this the awakening.

AMINA. Your story is indeed most wondrous. But dear Rodolphe, I tremble for your life. If you should be discovered the vengeance of the ruthless Wolfenstein, backed by his horde of fierce retainers would be terrible.

RODOLPHE. Fear not, I will defend my right with my life. The same kind power that interposed between me and destruction protect us still. You shall be saved. All is ready for our flight. On the border of the forest, beyond the boundary of the gardens, swift horses are concealed. After midnight the moon veiling her face behind the bracken, will cast a deep shadow over the valley. When it is quiet I will be beneath your window. The rest is easy. Carline and my faithful Greppo will accompany us.

AMINA. *(Throwing her arms around him.)* Oh, my Rodolphe, my more than life, coming this suddenly from the darkness of my despair into the sunlight of this new-born hope has dazzled me. My eyelids close. I cannot look this great joy in the face. I fear to call it mine.

RODOLPHE. Fear?

AMINA. Fear with that fear that springs from woman's love.

RODOLPHE. *(Kissing her.)* Be calm, sweet love, be brave, and all will yet be well. *(Music piano. Laughter heard outside at back.)* Hark, the masquers come this way. Let's mingle with the throng.

> *(They mask and cross to away. Music louder. MASQUERS enter laughing and chatting, remaining at back. While so engaged and after all are on, Music changes to hurry. HERTZOG with drawn sword enters hurriedly at terrace, followed by guards, WOLFENSTEIN with drawn sword, WULFGAR, BRUNO and VON PUFF with BARBARA, the two latter remaining on terrace. HERTZOG down right glaring on RODOLPHE.)*

WOLFENSTEIN. *(Center foot of terrace steps.)* Let no one stir; guard every avenue that leads from hence. *(To guests.)* Bear with me, friends, there's treason in our midst.

ALL. Treason?

WOLFENSTEIN. 'Tis said a serf, a wretch, usurping the semblance of a noble prince and bent on outrage has dared to mingle with this goodly throng. If that be false to all I'll make amends for this rude breaking in upon the general joy. If it be true 'tis fit we know it. Therefore I do command that all shall here unmask.

AMINA. Lost, lost.

ALL. Aye, let all unmask.

(All unmask. RODOLPHE in doing so, throws off his domino, draws his sword, and places himself before AMINA. Chord.)

WOLFENSTEIN. 'Tis true; yield, audacious miscreant!

RODOLPHE. Never, while life remains!

WOLFENSTEIN. Upon him, guards, hew him to pieces!

(Music. LADIES scream. AMINA faints and falls into the arms of GREPPO who enters. WOLFENSTEIN and GUARDS are rushing upon RODOLPHE.)

GREPPO. The ring, master, the ring.

(RODOLPHE kisses the ring. Foot, border and wing lights flashed quickly up. STALACTA springs from left in glittering mail, with helmet, sword and shield, followed by DRAGONFIN, armed with a trident. FAIRIES and NYMPHS as Amazons with breast plates, helmets, shields and javelins. GNOMES and AMPHIBEA with knotted clubs and tridents form on terrace right and left. WOLFENSTEIN, GUARDS and GENTLEMEN shrink back appalled. HERTZOG stands the embodiment of baffled rage. VON PUFF on terrace faints and falls into the arms of BARBARA, who fans him. Note—from the cue "Hew him to pieces," the whole action is hurried and simultaneous. Foot and stage lights flashed quickly up when RODOLPHE kisses the ring. When curtain drops first time, hold the picture to answer encore.

Quick Curtain

Act Four

Scene 1

An apartment in the castle of Wolfenstein. Six months later.

Music. Enter BARBARA.

BARBARA. Alas that things ever fall so ill. 'Tis now siz months since that never-to-be-forgotten night, and still no news of the lost mistress of Wolfenstein. Nor yet of his lordship who has sworn an oath never to return to the castle until he has brought her back and revenged himself on the horrible monster who has stolen her. And that graceless baggage Carline, too, to go off at the same time, leaving all the woes of the household to fall on my poor shoulders. And then to make matters worse, spells and witchcraft turn all things upside down. The cows milk vinegar, the wells are dry, the hens lay addled eggs—

VON PUFF. *(Entering right with very red nose and tipsy.)* And all the wine's turned sour.

BARBARA. *(Looking ruefully at him.)* There's another comfort. To think that I, the right honorable foster-mother that was to have been to her right honorable ladyship that was to have been, for whom many a young and tender heart has sighed in vain, should ever have thrown herself away upon a wine-butt.

VON PUFF. Hic! A wine-butt, Madam Von Puffengruntz?

BARBARA. Aye, a wine-butt, a beer barrel, a brute that hasn't drawn a sober breath since the day after we were married, now more than three months ago.

VON PUFF. Hic! A beer-barrel?

BARBARA. *(Savagely.)* I said a beer-barrel.

VON PUFF. Hic! Certainly, of course, just whichever you please, my dear, wine-butt or beer-barrel, it's all the same to me. You know you will cackle.

BARBARA. Cackle!

VON PUFF. Hic! Cackle, my dear. You know I never have a moment's peace. You're not even quiet when you're asleep. You snore, Madam Von Puffengrunz, you snore, loud enough to split the drum of my ear and rip up the seam up my nightcap.

BARBARA. Snore, you wretch, I snore?

VON PUFF. Hic! Yes, my dear, and have the nightmare. Hic! I don't like a wife that snores and I hate a wife that has the nightmare. In future I'm going to have separate apartments. Hereafter I intend to sleep alone.

BARBARA. Alone.

VON PUFF. Hic! I said alone.

BARBARA. Am I awake? Who and what do you take me for?

VON PUFF. Hic! I took you for a gentle spice-a sort of seasoning to the dull life I led here in the castle, but damn it, Madam, you've turned out to be all the condiments in one, a bottom layer of mustard, a top dressing of cayenne pepper and a subterranean lake of vinegar in the middle.

BARBARA. *(Enraged, approaching; he retreats around left.)* Cackle! Snore! Nightmare, separate apartments! Cayenne pepper? You wretch! You sot, you villain. I'll pepper you! *(Pulls his wig off.)* There, take that and that and that.

(Beats him over the head with it until both off stage.)

Curtain

Act Four

Scene 2

The retreat of Rodolphe in the forest of Bohemia.

Music. Distant sound of hunter's horn and echo. RODOLPHE and AMINA enter, followed by GREPPO. The former two are in hunting costume.

RODOLPHE. *(Throwing his spear and horn to GREPPO.)* I weary with the chase. Call together our people and bid them lead our horses to where the forest path crosses the brook- there we will join them.

GREPPO. 'Tis wisely resolved, good master. The sun declines, night comes on apace and we are yet some three good miles from home. Besides I'm hollow as a drum. Moreover, in early autumn venison keeps not overlong and the fat haunch of yonder noble buck cries out for speedy roasting. Pray do not tarry long.

(He exits.)

RODOLPHE. Well, dear love, tomorrow ends the year of our probation. Tomorrow, at the holy altar's foot, I call you mine.

AMINA. Tomorrow! How brief the time and yet how long 'till then. Oh, Rodolphe, will it come to us? There seems to be a lurking danger in the air--a cloud between us and the coming light.

RODOLPHE. Fear not. Here in the deep seclusion of our forest home we are safe from all pursuit. *(Distant horn and echo.)* Hark, 'tis Greppo calling in the huntsmen. Let's on to meet him.

(Music. They are crossing to right when they are suddenly confronted by HERTZOG, WOLFENSTEIN and WULFGAR, who enter quickly. Chord.)

WOLFENSTEIN. Ha, ha, ha! At last we meet!

RODOLPHE. *(Starting back and drawing his sword.)* Fly, Amina, seek safety with our people. My arm shall bar pursuit.

AMINA. No, Rodolphe, we will die together.

WOLFENSTEIN. Alive, take him alive! Yield!

RODOLPHE. *(Standing on his defense.)* He who takes my sword must win it.

HERTZOG. Put up thy blade; she whom thou would'st invoke is powerless to aid.

RODOLPHE. False wretch, but that another life hangs on the slender thread of mine—though coward numbers swarmed on every side—I'd try this issue with my single sword. But know thou still art juggled with. The power I once invoked is potent still. *(Music. He kisses the ring. STALACTA springs from thicket in glittering full armor, DRAGONFIN on from left.)* Behold, we meet on equal ground!

WOLFENSTEIN. Though environed by a thousand fiends my hate would find a way to reach you.

(*Music. Grand triple sword combat:* RODOLPHE *and* WOLFENSTEIN: DRAGONFIN *and* WULFGAR: STALACTA *and* HERTZOG. WOLFENSTEIN *and* WULFGAR *are slain.* HERTZOG *wounded and dismayed flees.* AMINA, *who during the combat has knelt in prayer, throws herself into the arms of* RODOLPHE. *Both kneel at the feet of* STALACTA. DRAGONFIN *indulges in grotesque exultation over the bodies of* WOLFENSTEIN *and* WULFGAR.)

Curtain

Act Four

Scene 3

The Forest.

Enter RODOLPHE *RH supporting* AMINA.

RODOLPHE. Look up, Amina, all danger's past. Courage, ere long, we'll meet our people.

AMINA. And you are safe?

RODOLPHE. Safe! Come, poor trembling dove. Courage, courage.

(*Exeunt. Music. Enter* HERTZOG, *infuriate.*)

HERTZOG. Let one vast curse fill all the air! Am I then juggled with! Malignant powers, obey your master's call. Viewless spirits of evil, work now your direst spells! As toppling mountains crush the mighty pines, crush thou the power that thwarts and mocks me. Zamiel, mighty master, I invoke thy aid.

(*Music. Thunder. Two* FIENDS *enter quickly right and left, bearing lighted flambeaux.*)

FIENDS. Your will?

HERTZOG. Summon your infernal legions—pursue yon flying pair. Fire the forest, girdle them with a belt of flame; close every avenue of escape. Away, away!

(*Music. Thunder.* FIENDS *rush off, followed by* HERTZOG.)

Curtain

Act Four

Scene 4

Burning forest.

A grand and comprehensive conflagration scene. Lights down. Music at rise. Loud crackling noise and red fire on both sides. RODOLPHE *and* AMINA *enter as they attempt to escape they are driven back by fiends with flaming torches.*

AMINA. *(In agony.)* I burn! I suffocate!

RODOLPHE. Courage, courage. The ring, the ring!

> *(He kisses the ring; Gong sounds; a rock opens disclosing a grotto of silver stalactites. They quickly enter.* HERTZOG *and the* FIENDS *spring forward, when* STALACTA *steps forward from the opening, holding aloft a glittering cross.* HERTZOG *and the* FIENDS *shrink back.)*

Tableau

Curtain

Act Four

Scene 5

The forest at night.

Lights down. Sound of hunter's horn and very faint echo. GREPPO *enters.*

GREPPO. What's the use? Now what is the use? The oftener I call, the fainter comes the answer. Here it is quite dark, Master waiting for the horses and I wandering about like a jack o' lantern, following the horn of some goblin huntsman. There's some devil's work going on. *(Starting.)* I beg his infernal

The Black Crook

Majesty's pardon; I hope I haven't said anything to offend, but strange sights and sounds are in the air. Birds that ought to have gone to roost an hour ago fly screaming from tree to tree. The dismal screech-owl, from his hole in the oak answers to the croak of the dreary monk-raven and just now I saw a big fat buck scampering through the forest with his tail on fire. Oh, dear, oh dear, what fearful omens. And I'm to be married tomorrow. If anything should happen to me—if my poor dear little Carline should happen to be left a widow before she's made a wife—if I should never taste—that is, if I should never know--Oh, Lord, it won't bear thinking of. I'll try once more. *(Winds the horn. Echo without scarily audible.)* Worse and worse. Oh Lord, Oh Lord. I want to go home.

(He exits.)

Curtain

Act Four

Scene 6

Pandemonium.

ZAMIEL in council, seated on an illuminated throne of skulls and flame at back center. To the right and left are lesser thrones, that on the right occupied by REDGLARE, with pen and open book, that on the left by a SECRETARY writing. At the foot of the central throne TWO DWARF-DEMONS, pages with wands in attendance. Music at rise. FIENDS discovered in a chorus of demoniacal yells and fiendish laughter, dancing around a flashing chasm. After the action is continued a brief time, ZAMIEL waves his sceptre. DEMONS separate and form right and left.

ZAMIEL. 'Tis well. Let silence reign awhile. How stands the record of the dying year? Has every seed brought sinful fruit? Is all the harvest gathered in—is every bond fulfilled?

REDGLARE. All! All save one.

ZAMIEL. Who plays the laggard?

REDGLARE. One who sought to rival thy great power; Hertzog, the Black Crook.

ALL THE FIENDS. Ho, ho, go.

(Echoed without and above, followed by a single wild blast of infernal music.)

ZAMIEL. If, when the brazen tongue of clamorous time, now trembling on the midnight verge, proclaims the appointed hour, the wail of the fresh soul by him betrayed, breaks on the air of hell, let him be summoned.

(Music. The DEMONS utter a wild wail of delight and resume the dance; the gong strikes twelve. At the first stroke, the DEMONS cease dancing and hold separate pictures of exultation. At the termination of each stroke loud and continued thunder; demons utter a wild cry. ZAMIEL rises and waves his sceptre. If possible the scene breaks away and discloses vistas of Pandemonium teeming with infernal life and wreaths of flame, from which appear illuminated heads of demons, skeletons, and nondescript monsters. Gong sounds. HERTZOG is dragged on by FIENDS and is dashed into the flaming chasm. DEMONS howl and dance around until:)

Curtain

Act Four

Scene 7

Subterranean gallery of emerald and crystal stalactites.

Music at rise. Characteristic march. Grand procession of AMPHIBEA and GNOMES bearing in their arms and upon their heads salvers and shells and quaint vases filled with gold and jewels. They are followed by AMAZONS in armor, led by STALACTA. They march from left to right, doubling the march and varying the evolutions until the transformation is ready when they exit and the scene breaks slowly away to:

Act Four

Scene 8

Realms of Stalacta.

Music at opening. An elaborate mechanical and scenically construction of the realms of Stalacta, occupying the entire stage. This scene must be of gradually developing and culminating beauty, introducing during its various scenes, STALACTA, the entire host of fairies, sprites, water nymphs, amphibea, gnomes, etc., bearing treasure. RODOLPHE and AMINA, GREPPO and CARLINE. Calcium lights, brilliant fires and:

Slow Curtain

END

Made in the USA
Monee, IL
07 January 2023